REDWOOD CURTAIN

BY LANFORD WILSON

★

DRAMATISTS
PLAY SERVICE
INC.

★

REDWOOD CURTAIN
Copyright © 1993, 1995, Lanford Wilson

All Rights Reserved

SPECIAL NOTE
Anyone receiving permission to produce REDWOOD CURTAIN is required to give credit to the Author as sole and exclusive Author of the Play on the title page of all programs distributed in connection with performances of the Play and in all instances in which the title of the Play appears for purposes of advertising, publicizing or otherwise exploiting the Play and/or a production thereof. The name of the Author must appear on a separate line, in which no other name appears, immediately beneath the title and in size of type equal to 50% of the largest, most prominent letter used for the title of the Play. No person, firm or entity may receive credit larger or more prominent than that accorded the Author.

SPECIAL NOTE ON SONGS AND RECORDINGS
For performance of the songs, arrangements and recordings mentioned in this Play that are protected by copyright, the permission of the copyright owners must be obtained; or other songs, arrangements and recordings in the public domain substituted.

For Rod Marriott

With grateful thanks to Michael Baird, David Kahn, Don Speziale, Lisa Gayton, Rich Remedios, Seattle Rep, Circle Rep Playwrights Lab and the usual suspects: Michael, Marshall, Fred, Claris, Debra, Tanya and Loren Dunlap forever for the rubber squirrel.

REDWOOD CURTAIN was produced by Seattle Repertory Company (Daniel Sullivan, Artistic Director), in conjunction with Circle Repertory Company (Tanya Berezin, Artistic Director), in Seattle, Washington, on January 8, 1992. It was directed by Marshall W. Mason; the scene design was by John Lee Beatty; the costume design was by Laura Crow; the lighting design was by Dennis Parichy; the sound design was by Chuck London and Stewart Werner; the original music was composed by Peter Kater and the stage manager was Fred Reinglas. The cast was as follows:

LYMAN .... David Morse
GERI .... Kimiko Cazanov
GENEVA .... Debra Monk

REDWOOD CURTAIN was produced by Philadelphia Drama Guild (Mary B. Robinson, Artistic Director), in association with the Annenberg Center, in Philadelphia, Pennsylvania, on March 6, 1992. It was directed by Marshall W. Mason; the scene design was by John Lee Beatty; the costume design was by Laura Crow; the lighting design was by Dennis Parichy; the sound design was by Chuck London and Stewart Werner; the original music was composed by Peter Kater and the production stage managers were Fred Reinglas and Roy W. Backes. The cast was as follows:

LYMAN .... Steve Bassett
GERI .... Kimiko Cazanov
GENEVA .... Debra Monk

REDWOOD CURTAIN was produced by Old Globe Theatre (Jack O'Brien, Artistic Director), in San Diego, California, on January 21, 1993. It was directed by Marshall W. Mason; the scene design was by John Lee Beatty; the costume design was by Laura Crow; the lighting design was by Dennis Parichy; the sound design was by Chuck London and Stewart Werner; the original music was composed by Peter Kater and the production stage manager was Fred Reinglas. The cast was as follows:

LYMAN ....Jeff Daniels
GERI ....Sung Yun Cho
GENEVA ....Debra Monk

REDWOOD CURTAIN was produced on Broadway by Robert Cole, Benjamin Mordecai, Deborah D. Mathews, James M. Nederlander, James D. Stern, William P. Suter and Circle Repertory Company (Tanya Berezin, Artistic Director), at the Brooks Atkinson Theatre, in New York City, on March 30, 1993. It was directed by Marshall W. Mason; the scene design was by John Lee Beatty; the costume design was by Laura Crow; the lighting design was by Dennis Parichy; the sound design was by Chuck London and Stewart Werner; the original music was composed by Peter Kater and the production stage manager was Fred Reinglas. The cast was as follows:

LYMAN ....Jeff Daniels
GERI ....Sung Yun Cho
GENEVA ....Debra Monk

CHARACTERS

LYMAN FELLERS is 38, a veteran of the Vietnam War. He is a large, strong man. He has a stubble of beard and long unkempt hair.

GERI RIORDAN is a 17-year-old Asian-American girl. She may be a little more than the 88 pounds she claims, but she is small. She has long black hair. She is quite straightforward, sure of herself and totally American.

GENEVA SIMONSON is in her mid-40s, smart, well-spoken and a little American Western in speech and dress.

THE SCENE

Scene 1: A Redwood Forest near Arcata, California, in the Northwestern part of the state.

Scene 2: Briefly a car. The Music Room of Geneva's home in Arcata.

Scene 3: A Coffee House, The Forest, The Music Room.

It is not necessary for these locations to be depicted realistically. The simpler, the better.

TIME

Late June, 1990.

REDWOOD CURTAIN should be performed without intermission.

REDWOOD CURTAIN

SCENE ONE

2:00 pm. A forest of extremely large first growth redwoods.

Lyman is a large strong man with a stubble of beard and longish unkempt hair. He wears two pairs of pants and two sweaters over a shirt. He carries a knapsack. He is unwashed. His voice is low and raspy, rather rough. He seldom smiles and never laughs. His eyes, while alert, are dull. He is 38.

A dog is yelping excitedly, chasing a rabbit in the distance.

LYMAN. *(Yelling encouragement.)* Go go go go! Get him! Catch that mother! *(He drops his knapsack to the ground.)* Useless bitch. Better be a damn moose, both of us eat. *(He sits, then yells again.)* Stop yappin', bitch. Do it! *(To himself.)* Don't come whining back here. *(After a moment Geri, an Asian-American girl of 17, can be seen, as far away as possible, silently watching Lyman. How long has she been there? She moves closer now. She is in a position where she can be seen, but he gives no indication of her presence. Geri is small, straight forward and totally American.)*
GERI. Excuse me. *(Beat.)* Could you tell me where the path is? *(She watches him a moment. Nothing.)* If you could just indicate the general direction back to civilization. I've got myself turned around here. *(Pause.)* Mister? *(Pause. Lyman begins digging in his knapsack for something; he seems to have withdrawn into himself.)* I know you can talk, I heard you yelling to your dog. *(She stays some distance from him. From the other direction the dog has begun yelping again.)*
LYMAN. *(Jumping up, yelling.)* Get him, get to it, bitch, go! *(He sits back down.)*

GERI. *(After a moment.)* What's his name?

LYMAN. You got a dollar?

GERI. What?

LYMAN. You got a dollar on you?

GERI. No, I don't. What a great turnoff. That really says get out of my face, doesn't it? That must be effective. I didn't bring any money with me this morning. I was just going for a walk. I made the mistake of losing the path. I thought I saw a banana slug. They're supposed to be thick up here, I haven't seen one. Then I kept going like an idiot and got a little lost. *(Beat.)* If you can be a little lost. If you could just point —

LYMAN. You ask the wrong questions. Little girl. Hang on that purse, must be something in it.

GERI. Yeah, well, my whole life is in it, but I didn't bring any money. Really. It's just I have this terrible sense of direction. I mean it isn't difficult finding your way into the woods, but … *(This dumb place.)* I tried looking for moss. It's supposed to grow on the North side of trees, you can use it like a compass. Unfortunately it's so wet up here the moss grows all the way around the trees. One for the moss. *(Pause. She is looking up into the trees, leaning against one.)* They're something else, though, aren't they? They're amazing. I wouldn't have believed it. I keep leaning up against them, maybe I'll draw some strength from them. Or perspective. Whatever it is they have. Something. I don't think it's working. This forest is over 20 thousand years old. These trees were standing here before Egypt built pyramids or the Valley of Kings. They were already the oldest living thing on earth when Jesus was born. *(The hound, way off, begins yapping again.)* Which kinna makes me feel, hey, you know, great. One for the redwood. But, I mean we're talking early retirement at 55? Give me a break.

LYMAN. *(Jumping up, yelling after the dog.)* Give up, bitch! You're beat! He's got ya! Pitch it, bitch! *(Geri has started at his sudden movement. He sits back down.)*

GERI. *(After a moment.)* Of course I don't know what direction Arcata is from here. I mean North, South, East or West. So it wouldn't be much help to have a compass. It might keep me from going around in circles. In a labyrinth you're supposed to take *every turn* and always turn left and you'll find your way out. I can't wait to try it. That's the sort of knowledge that doesn't help you when you're lost in a redwood forest. Wow! I love the sound of that. Redwood Forest.

LYMAN.   You won't find your way out from here. You're gonna die here.

GERI.   *(Beat.)* Well, okay. I guess that's possible. There's always a first time for everything. *(Lyman has found a package of Bamboo papers in his knapsack. He begins rolling a joint.)* Actually it wouldn't be the first time. I was in a bike accident when I was 12. One of my neighbors gave me a joy ride on his Harley and ran us into the side of a pickup carrying cantaloupes. I think he'd been trying to impress his girlfriend. Apparently it worked, she married him. I was on the operating table for 7 hours. My spine and left hip were partially crushed. Only when they gave me the anesthetic my heart stopped for 22 seconds. I didn't see the Terrible Bright White Light at the End of the Tunnel. *(She shrugs.)* Everybody asks. Sometimes I say I did, because when I say I didn't they think I wasn't really dead. I asked my doctor if I really was dead for 22 seconds and he said you really were dead for 22 seconds. So I asked him for a death certificate to prove it, but he wouldn't give me one. *(Beat.)* All these malpractice suits probably. *(Beat.)* I imagine you saw a lot of that, huh? *(Beat.)* Death.

LYMAN.   Shit.

GERI.   Yeah. Are you gonna light that joint or what? *(As she starts to reach toward the joint Lyman makes a grab for her purse. Geri jumps aside. There is a flash of lightning, a roll of thunder. Lyman looks around him in dismay.)* Hey, you! Come on, guy! Watch it! I can take care of myself. *(Quickly improvising.)* I mean, uh ... I'm a black belt in karate.

LYMAN.   Never tell your opponent what he's up against.

GERI.   Yeah, well, I believe in fair warning.

LYMAN.   Don't show your hand.

GERI.   Just believe it.

LYMAN.   What do you want from me?

GERI.   Listen, I was just on a little expedition to look at the plant life. I study botany. Most of this stuff I've never seen before.

LYMAN.   Bullshit. I thought you were looking for slugs.

GERI.   We don't have redwoods where I live. Or ferns like these. I know their botanical name, I just can't remember it right now.

LYMAN.   You always carry your purse in the woods?

GERI.   It was a spur of the moment decision.

LYMAN.   You wear sneakers and shorts, dress like that on a hike?

GERI.   God, it was a whim! I wasn't planning to rappel mountains or anything.

LYMAN.   Who do you think you're talking to?

GERI.   I have no idea, I was just —

LYMAN.   — With your black belt in karate and your sneakers and shorts. You think I'm deaf? I look blind to you?

GERI.   I'm not really putting together what it is that you're trying to say.

LYMAN.   *You been following me for the last two hours! (A long pause.)*

GERI.   Well, you were yelling, I could hardly keep from hearing you.

LYMAN.   I was standing on G Street, you came out of your yogurt milk shake shop, you followed me a mile up 101, you followed me into the trees, you followed me along the dry creek, you followed me up the hill, you followed me around the fern walley. Now you're lost, aren't you? You don't know where the fuck you are.

GERI.   Well, just because I say something, actually, doesn't necessarily mean I mean it. I mean I'm a terrible liar.

LYMAN.   Nobody can lie to me. I don't hear them. You can't be lied to if you don't listen.

GERI.   *(She takes this quite seriously.)* I'll bet you don't, either. What do you hear?

LYMAN.   They got all you college jerks looking in the woods for everybody's plants. Get your neck broke for you is what you'll get.

GERI.   I don't believe I know what you're saying.

LYMAN.   You're not dumb. Come in here, think I'm gonna lead you to something. Come back and pull up my plants. Turn in my name. Just go on.

GERI.   Oh, I'm with you. You're talking contraband. I don't want your marijuana plants if that's what you're saying. They'll have to legalize it eventually.

LYMAN.   You in school here?

GERI.   They're supposed to have one of the best horticulture departments in the country. Fruit trees and all that. It's a little agrarian for what I want, but I figure I'll go two years and transfer.

LYMAN.   Let me see your I.D.

GERI.   My what?

LYMAN.   Your school I.D.

GERI.   Back at the dorm.

LYMAN.   Throw it over here.

GERI.   I don't have it on me.

LYMAN.   Give it here, damnit.

GERI.   I'm not carrying it, I said. Jesus.

LYMAN.   If you don't give me your school I.D., I'm gonna take the thing away from you.

GERI.   You don't frighten me.

LYMAN.   *(Getting up.)* Throw me your damn purse. Do it!

GERI.   *(Digging into her purse.)* Okay. Just sit down. God. *(She fishes her driver's license out of her wallet.)* I feel like I'm being carded. *(She pitches her license to him.)* That picture's awful.

LYMAN.   *(Reading.)* California. What's "La Jolly?"

GERI.   Well, you're not Spanish. You must belong to the other half of the country's population. La Jolla is a place north of San Diego. It may mean "jolly" for all I know. It isn't.

LYMAN.   Where's your student I.D., Geraldine Lon?

GERI.   Geri. Only they wouldn't let me put that on the license.

LYMAN.   What kind of name is Lon?

GERI.   That's my mother's name. Vietnamese. She was going to call me Farrow, which was dad's name but she looked

11

it up in the dictionary and it means "To give birth to a litter of pigs."

LYMAN. Toss over the wallet.

GERI. No. I mean it.

LYMAN. What you got from that school?

GERI. Nothing on me.

LYMAN. This isn't you. You're no 21. You don't go to that college either. How old are you?

GERI. I might have gone to school here. I considered it. You look at all of them. You go to these ridiculously over-endowed campuses in the middle of these poverty-stricken redneck towns, decide you wouldn't go there if it were the last school on earth, then they turn you down anyway. What Humboldt is really hot for is land management and conservation, which is something I just like respect the shit out of but it's not me. Could I have my driver's license back? *(A beat. Leveling with him.)* I came to Arcata to visit a friend of mom's, this professor. He teaches here. I'm staying with him and his wife.

LYMAN. What's his name?

GERI. You're familiar with the faculty? Dr. Smith. Really. Mathematics. Only not the interesting stuff; not theory or astrophysics or anything, so he's kinna dry but his wife is cool.

LYMAN. *(He holds up the license.)* You make that face on purpose? You thought that was cute?

GERI. We were all goofing. I don't like to have my picture taken. *(Beat.)* You should understand that.

LYMAN. Let me see your wallet.

GERI. I'd rather not.

LYMAN. Yeah? Hand it here.

GERI. No.

LYMAN. Why not?

GERI. Because it has all the money I have left for my whole vacation in it.

LYMAN. I could take it away from you.

GERI. No, you can't. You really can't. I can run faster than you can. Actually you get around the woods pretty well, but on 101 I could tell you still limp. When you're hustling the tourists you tell them you got shot up in Cambodia, but really you were passed out in Isaac Minor Alley and Buzz Warren ran his pick-up over your foot. He started to get out, your dog nearly took his leg off. Did you know that? 19 stitches and a rabies shot. You were howling so loud the neighbors called the cops. The police took you to the emergency room where you basically freaked. On the local skinny, Mrs. Smith is very up to speed.

LYMAN.   Take out the money and hand over the wallet.

GERI.   Except you. That's all she knew about you. *(A pause. He hands her the license. As she reaches for it he grabs her arm, whirls her around and though she tries several moves he has her down on her face on the ground with his foot in the middle of her back.)* You bastard! You're squashing my breasts, damnit. *(He takes the wallet from her bag, drops the bag beside her and steps off.)* Just take the money and give me my wallet. Don't paw my things.

LYMAN.   *(Thumbing through the money.)* Jesus Christ, haven't you ever heard of Traveler's Cheques?

GERI.   All the tellers at my bank suck. Now give me my damn wallet. *(And she flies at him. There is a huge scuffle during which she gets in one really solid jab to the gut, enough to make us believe she might really know the rudiments of karate, but she ends up face down in the dirt again with him sitting on her butt.)*

LYMAN.   Are you gonna act nice? Are you gonna act nice?

GERI.   Could you put that some other way?

LYMAN.   Are you gonna act nice?

GERI.   Sure. *(He gets off her back. She rolls over.)* I'm dead. *(Quite angry.)* I told you I've got a bad back. I've got a plastic hip and a steel rod in my spine. I can't fight. I weigh 88 pounds. What the hell are you doing? I'm frail, stupid!

LYMAN.   I didn't believe you.

GERI.   That part was true. I thought you didn't hear people. You were too busy marching to the beat of your own drum or something.

LYMAN.   *(Beat. He is looking through her wallet.)* You got your whole life in here, huh? *(Beat.)* I could leave you here, you'd die.

GERI. *(Still flushed.)* I have an infallible sense of direction. It's uncanny. I'm part cat or something.

LYMAN. Which way is Arcata?

GERI. *(She points back and to the right.)* About 6 miles that way. The last hour we've been going around in circles. What, were you trying to confuse me? I thought you were losing it.

LYMAN. You lie about everything?

GERI. The truth isn't all it's cracked up to be. I don't know how lying got such a bad rap. Could you give me that back, please? It makes me incredibly nervous to see someone pawing it. Really.

LYMAN. I don't believe your reallys anymore.

GERI. You are such a total troll. I was embarrassed following you, the way you stomp through the woods like a rhino or something. You don't even feel the enchantment, do you? I probably should teach you a lesson. You've limited yourself to such a physical, blundering oafdom that you can actually sit talking to a sylph and not even know it.

LYMAN. A what?

GERI. A nymph, a sylph. Actually more of a genie.

LYMAN. In shorts and sneakers?

GERI. I just threw something on! You couldn't lose me in the woods. The deer would guide me out. I could make the whole woods vanish if I wanted. If I were in danger the trees would bend down so I could clasp their highest bough then they'd swing up and throw me to safety. I'm just lucky you didn't ask me where I keep my pot of gold. When we're helpless we're compelled to reveal its hiding place.

LYMAN. That's a leprechaun. *(He holds up a picture from her wallet, just flashing it, he doesn't take it from it's sleeve.)* Who's that?

GERI. Me and a couple of girlfriends. The blonde actually got married last week. Which is like unbelievable because she is the most totally user-friendly girl in class. To some geek from Bakersfield. And will be living there if you can believe it. I wouldn't have followed you at all if I'd known you'd pull that Rambo macho crap.

LYMAN. What's that?

GERI. Trying to act like some damn Rambo or somebody.

LYMAN. Who's he?

GERI. You can't mean it. I'd willingly trade places with anyone alive who'd never heard that name. A bullshit green beret in the movies. He's sent back to Nam, like this one-man army, to rescue a group of MIAs. And before he leaves, you'll like this, he says to his captain, "Yo, are they gonna let us win this time?" The movie house goes wild. Suddenly everyone realizes the only way our boys could have lost is if someone wouldn't let them win. We were double-crossed. Have you been away so long you don't know you're a hero now? Come home, all is forgiven. We don't have a Vietnam Syndrome anymore. Ollie-Ollie Oxen free, you guys. We win. It makes you wonder about all the wonderful wars we won.

LYMAN. *(He holds up another photo from the wallet.)* Who's that?

GERI. My mother.

LYMAN. Pretty.

GERI. I'll tell her. *(He holds up another and keeps it up.)* Do you mind? That's the woman who bought me from my real mother. Not a bad investment, but she has a nose for that sort of thing. I turned out to be this world class piano prodigy, probably worth a fortune. 'Course she's a billionaire, money means nothing to those people. And if you believe that she has a race horse she'd like to sell you. *(He continues to hold the photo up.)* Her name's Julia. She's my foster mother or adopted mother or whatever you call it. She's my mother, she's just not related to me.

LYMAN. *(He goes back to the other woman.)* Who's this other one then?

GERI. That's my real mother only I've never met her.

LYMAN. How you going to tell her I said she was pretty?

GERI. Okay, I won't. Would you give me that back, please? *(He holds up another. Beat.)* Julia's husband. Laird Alfred Leslie Riordan. "Alfred Leslie" because he claimed to be related to the composer Erik Alfred Leslie Satie. He was my foster father. Died 2 years ago. Taught me all the usual parlor tricks — play an instrument, jump through hoops, roller skate. All the stuff that kept people entertained at dinner parties so he could concentrate on his drinking. Laird was the only desk-jockey lieutenant, didn't see a day's fighting, to come completely unglued in the war. Came back and drank himself totally into the toilet. *(He holds up another.)* Boy. Lives across the street.

LYMAN. Aw, Your boyfriend.

GERI. It's seriously frowned on for nymphs to get involved with mortals. It's been known to happen but the results are inevitably a disaster.

LYMAN. Who's the GI? *(A long pause.)*

GERI. *(Very level.)* I think that's you. *(A long silent pause, Lyman looks at photo.)* You're so small in the picture you can't really tell, can you? Taken 17 years ago in Saigon. Private Ray Farrow. You signed the papers for mother and me to get out, letter of intent, whatever, then about when we got on the boat, you took a train North from San Francisco. The last time anyone heard from you was four years ago, south of here, in Hopland. You weren't carrying an I.D., but they knew you from your description. Can't mess around in Hopland. That's wine country. They run a model community. The sheriff told you to get out of town. Said you hadn't shaved for a month, looked like a good candidate for the Redwood Curtain.

LYMAN. *(A beat. He throws her wallet back to her, rather roughly.)* Not me. I didn't fraternize.

GERI. Is that what they call it.

LYMAN. I didn't go with prostitutes.

GERI. Mother owned a florist shop in Saigon.

LYMAN. Pretty stupid to leave that.

GERI. With me on the way? They'd have killed her probably. I imagine she'd seen what they did to those who "fraternized" with the French. She's probably done well here.

LYMAN. Drives a stiff bargain.

GERI. Shrewd cookie.

LYMAN. Hard as nails.

GERI. Inscrutable.

LYMAN. Where is she now?

GERI. No idea. *(Pause.)*

LYMAN. Why me?

GERI. I thought I recognized you.

LYMAN. You even know your dad?

GERI. I thought you recognized me.

LYMAN. Never saw you before.

GERI. Neither has my father. I don't think he knows I exist. Day before yesterday. I saw you standing on the street with your dog. We passed each other and you looked right into my face. I think you saw it then. I did.

LYMAN. Saw what?

GERI. Look into my eyes.

LYMAN. Come on.

GERI. What's wrong?

LYMAN. I saw that genie stuff over there.

GERI. I come from a very magical culture.

LYMAN. I know.

GERI. Don't look down. What do you see? We control the elements. *(It begins to grow dark.)* I can gather the clouds from far out at sea and pile them over these woods. I could call upon the air for violence and destruction. *(It is very dark, lightning flashes, a rolling thunder runs over the woods.)* I could will it to rain or thin the turbulence, send the clouds out over the ocean and inform the sun to burn through the fog and warm the earth. *(The sun breaks through the clouds and shines brightly.)* I can tell the birds to fly to the trees that surround the vineyards across the valley and leave the woods to the two of us. *(Birds call: a light sifting of dry needles falls as they fly off, their calls fading.)* Except for the eagle. He protects me. He'll stay. *(An eagle calls. The sun continues to shine brightly through the redwoods.)* What's your name?

LYMAN. *(After a pause, still looking at her.)* One of your eyes is gray.

GERI. Almost blue.

LYMAN. One is just a normal gook eye, black. The other one is gray.

GERI. That occurs once in ten million. Same odds as the Lottery.

LYMAN. With mixed blood you're liable to get anything.

GERI. And you. Your eyes are dull, aren't they? They've seen a lot, haven't they? But it's still discernible. One of your eyes is blue and the other is brown.

LYMAN.   Not so anybody would notice.

GERI.   Americans don't look each other in the eye for all our straightforwardness.

LYMAN.   You consider yourself American?

GERI.   You kidding? I was adopted into one of the Former Top Ten Families of California. I just don't know where I was born. Somewhere in the old country. To an estranged mother and a father wandering around Eureka, California in the fog. With one blue eye and one brown.

LYMAN.   *(Beat.)* Not me.

GERI.   How much do you remember?

LYMAN.   Not a lot. Too much. Not everything.

GERI.   A young woman named Lily?

LYMAN.   I didn't mess with many of the locals much. You couldn't trust them.

GERI.   I wonder why.

LYMAN.   I didn't care.

GERI.   Let me see your I.D.

LYMAN.   Don't carry one.

GERI.   Sure you do.

LYMAN.   I'm not your dad, don't worry about it.

GERI.   What's your name? Do you know?

LYMAN.   What was his?

GERI.   I told you. Ray Farrow.

LYMAN.   Say it again.

GERI.   Ray Farrow.

LYMAN.   No. *(Pause.)*

GERI.   Did you know him?

LYMAN.   I wouldn't remember. What division was he in?

GERI.   Infantry.

LYMAN.   I was a combat engineer.

GERI.   What do they do?

LYMAN.   Blow up bridges.

GERI.   My dad wanted to be a builder. You were studying architecture.

LYMAN.   No.

GERI.   What then?

LYMAN.   I don't know, kid.

GERI.   Where was school?

LYMAN.   I don't think about it.

GERI.   Where are you from? Where did you grow up? What kind of car did you drive around the town square? Who were the girls who wouldn't let you in? You joined the army because they told you you could choose your own training.

LYMAN.   *(He looks at her a moment.)* Some joker came to our school, said enlist for 3 years, choose your A.I.T. I said I wanted engineering. They said, great, combat engineering. Blow up everything an engineer builds.

GERI.   *(Beat.)* What rank were you?

LYMAN.   E4. Special Engineer.

GERI.   Where are you from?

LYMAN.   It doesn't matter now. I don't remember.

GERI.   Nobody knows much about you. Or any of you. Maybe as long as you don't all murder them in their beds, they just count their blessings. You see homeless people, but you guys wandering around Arcata and Eureka are different, aren't you? "Eureka." Wow, is that ever wrong. What's Greek for "I've lost it?" I asked this reporter on the Arcata Union how many guys from Nam have drifted up here over the years, hiding out behind the Redwood Curtain. They don't even have a good estimate. Somewhere between three and maybe eight thousand. A lot of latitude there. All of you just move, float through town like specters. All you ghosts. Wandering around the streets, working odd jobs once a month, half high half the time, eating out of garbage pails and what you can hunt. Probably good hunters. Maybe you have a shack out here. Just a piece of tin to keep the rain off you and your dog. You wouldn't be cold with all those clothes. One of the guys I asked, why have so many of you come here? said it's a lot like Vietnam: quiet, beautiful, damp, the smell. Actually a lot of them have told me that. I've been looking for you for a long time. *(He stands and a spell seems to be broken.)*

LYMAN.   Sorry. Grew up in a city, no small town. No town square. Go on, now. Tell you something. Arcata's straight that way. *(He points D.L.)* Just take off, okay? Go on. Keep walking against the sun.

GERI.   The sun that I caused to shine.

LYMAN.   The fog burns off about this time every day.

GERI.   Arcata's that way? Boy. Just walk till I find it, huh? What if I didn't know? I really would get lost. What? Would that make your day or something? Knowing that I was wandering around lost at night? You and your dog could giggle over that, I guess.

LYMAN.   You leave, I'll never think another thing about it. I'll forget I ever saw you in 10 minutes. Guaranteed.

GERI.   That's just the way you are, huh? So you care that little about people, or do you just not retain things?

LYMAN.   Fine. Whatever. It's the way you said. Down there. Just go on.

GERI.   I mean, I don't know. Maybe you were shell-shocked or something. It clearly affected your mind somehow. I mean you're not what anyone would call remotely normal.

LYMAN.   Yeah? What's normal?

GERI.   No no no no, sorry. Normal, whatever it is, is something far less of a sociopath. I mean, forgive me if that's a surprise to you.

LYMAN.   *(More to himself, but aloud.)* First it's too damn cold, then it's too damn close. Fry your ass, boil or something. Hot as hell in here and still wet. *(He takes off one sweater then the other. He has on a T-shirt and a short sleeved shirt that expose his white biceps with a tattoo of an eagle.)*

GERI.   Oh, my god. Oh, my god. Oh, lord.

LYMAN.   What? What now? Just go on.

GERI.   Where did you get that tattoo? You have an eagle — Who are you? You tell me your name. Right now. *(She looks dizzy, she holds her head, trying to maintain her balance.)* Oh, god. Oh, lord. Oh, lord. *(She staggers a step, trying to straighten up and faints dead away on the forest floor. The man looks at her. It is very still. He picks up her wallet and looks through it. He takes a picture out, pulling it from the sleeve, looking on the back for an inscription. An eagle cries out. The man looks up against the sun, shading his eyes. The lights fade to black.)*

SCENE TWO

The stage is black except for the headlights of a Mercedes pointing directly at the audience, the beams angled below eye level. In the spill of the dash light is Geneva Simonson, a woman in her 40s, who is driving. Geri is in the passenger seat, wearing a man's winter jacket. She leans against the window, looking out into the dark. Most of the time Geneva manages to conceal her deep concern for Geri's wellbeing.

GENEVA.   You say you're fine, so I'll believe you're fine, but you don't look fine at all. Zip that up, love. I'm surprised you're not frozen. This isn't La Jolla. *(Geri zips up the jacket.)* You were in the woods. And some man was in the woods. And you fainted. Did he jump out from behind a tree and go, "Boo!"? I'm trying to construct a plausible scenario here. *(Beat.)* I hope to hell this wasn't another one of your "Father Candidates." You know how I feel about that. *(Nothing. More to herself than Geri.)* Nothing's more exasperating than a 17-year old-genius with magical powers who thinks she can take care of herself. Your mother would literally kill me. And I'd deserve it. Alone. In the woods. At night. Accosted by a man.
GERI.   I wasn't accosted, Aunt Geneva. I'm fine.
GENEVA.   *(A pause, she sighs.)* You never hear about night vapors anymore, but I'm sure that's what this is. The fog comes in across low tide and picks up that really pleasant smell of beached seaweed. Or an inland wind brings over the aroma of the pulp mills, and all the various chemicals involved in that fragrant enterprise. I don't suppose you struck out this morning with the intention of hiking all the way to some Tourist Trap T-shirt Emporium in the middle of the forest. *(Beat.)* If you'd been — what time was it? — another 15 minutes, those people would have closed and gone home. Just be thankful they had a phone, not all of them do.
GERI.   I'm sorry if I made you worry.

GENEVA.   *(A beat.)* Actually we never thought a thing about it. We thought you were at the movies. They don't get out for another hour. Barney left just before you called. Some last ditch effort with the lawyers. Alas. Would that he were shtupping his secretary, it'd be less a waste of time and god knows she needs it. But it just isn't in his nature. He's always put sex in the same general category as exercise. Too little reward for such great effort. *(She glances at Geri again.)* That was a joke. *(Beat.)* I'm trying to remember this one's name. The lawyer. He says we've already lost the company. It's refreshing to hear a lawyer tell the truth. We tried everything legal there was to try. The judges just struck us down. This outfit's going to clear-cut every tree in sight, they're going to come through here with buzz-saws. I just feel the trees screaming at me.
GERI.   I don't know why you're so scared of them. They're just trees. They won't bite you.
GENEVA.   I felt perfectly safe when I knew for sure they were mine. *(Beat.)* Dad taught Laird and me how to drive down here on this road before it was paved. In a '49 Packard. It was an old car, you understand. *(She looks at Geri, who doesn't respond, and deliberately changes the subject.)* I think I'm going to be after a spot of tea. How does that strike you?
GERI.   In bed maybe.
GENEVA.   Are you being glum and sulky or are you really not feeling well?
GERI.   I'm fine.
GENEVA.   I don't want you to get sick your last day here.
GERI.   I'm just angry. Disappointed in myself.
GENEVA.   Well, I'm almost never what I hope I'll be.
GERI.   My shoulder hurts. I think I fell on it funny.
GENEVA.   *(Not a criticism, almost a complaint.)* Nobody faints anymore. I don't think I ever have. I passed out cold once in the back seat of a car, but I was drunk. Four men in the car and not one of them took advantage of me. I wasn't always this beautiful. *(Beat.)* Are you hungry?
GERI.   No.
GENEVA.   Take a hot bath and I'll have Matilda bring your

22

tea up to your room. (*Pause. Then she sings a few lines from* "*Matilda, Matilda.*"*) I can never say her name without thinking of that.

GENEVA.   Why didn't you buy a sweat shirt in that place? You could keep warm at least.

GERI.   The bastard stole my wallet.

GENEVA.   Geri. Before you do anything call your mother and tell her to call the credit card people.

GERI.   Aunt Geneva, think. He couldn't possibly use them.

GENEVA.   He could sell them, or throw them away and someone else could find them. (*They reach their destination Geneva sighs and closes her eyes a moment. She reaches to turn off the car lights; they dim as Geri is getting out of the car. We hear the car doors slam in the darkness. They speak over the dark a moment.*) Tell Matilda to run your bath and I'll start the tea. And don't get exposure or something. I don't know how to treat it.

GERI.   No, I'm fine now. (*A piano is heard playing the last movement of the Waldstein sonata* as the lights come up the following morning on the music room of a large Victorian house. Geneva is listening to the tape of a recital. Geri enters as the movement ends.*) What are you doing in the music room?

GENEVA.   Don't turn it off, this is the best part.

GERI.   Thanks. (*There is a burst of applause and cheering on the stereo. Geri turns it off in the middle.*)

GENEVA.   It gives me goose bumps every time I hear it. That was San Diego.

GERI.   I dropped the F natural at the end of the last run.

GENEVA.   What's that note?

GERI.   There are a lot of them.

GENEVA.   The one you keep repeating. Bong, bong. You know what I mean. I become so sensitized to that note I can pick it out in a whole run. Which is what Beethoven intended,

---

* See Special Note on Songs and Recordings on copyright page.

23

I'm sure. Especially the way you bang on it. Where is it? Go play it.

GERI. No, Aunt Geneva.

GENEVA. Just that one note. *(Rather than argue, Geri goes to the piano and hits the G twice. Geneva groans in ecstasy.)*

GERI. Why anyone would want to be involved, even peripherally, with music is beyond me. Nobody *ever* listens. We go to the opera, everyone, I mean *everyone* is asleep. Music is Ovaltine to them. Mother had all these intellectual types over: she had some winner of the National Book Award and this critic and a physicist and this Genius Painter and God knows how many really good musicians you might actually learn something from. All they talked about all weekend was this concert. Zubin Mehta was guest conductor on *Live from London* or something, they all know him, of course. They go in the TV room, they turn on the TV, they start with the "He's let his hair grow. He looks very distinguished. I love his tails ..." and the architectural detail of Albert Hall, which they didn't even like and you couldn't see anyway, and all the music they've heard there, and how foul the food was at the "interval," and all the music they've heard all over Europe and the food they had *there,* and finally just the *food* they've had. They didn't hear a note of music.

GENEVA. You should have taped it.

GERI. The point was to hear it live from London. Also I don't know how to work the VCR. The one time I got it to tape anything I set it to record *Cheers;* I came home, I'd taped an entire Yankee–Oakland game. Also the program was "Mostly Mahler," which is not my idea of a fun evening.

GENEVA. You're sounding bitter.

GERI. You're darned right I'm bitter. I practice like a dog for 12 years, get exercised to tears over some nuance of theory for godsake over something nobody even hears. It's a rip-off. You know the average number of playing times for a CD? You don't, I read it last week — even pop records, the average number of times a record is played is one time and a quarter. And they want me to spend a week in some studio going over and over the "Goldberg Variations" — like we

24

need another recording of that? Forget it.

GENEVA. *(After a moment she lets that pass.)* Is that a good show, *Cheers?*

GERI. I love it, but I intend to marry Ted Danson. Do they really serve food during intermission at Albert Hall?

GENEVA. I imagine.

GERI. That is just so — typical. It's all Julia's friends talk about. During breakfast they talk about lunch; during lunch they start planning dinner.

GENEVA. Which Mahler?

GERI. The Seventh. In *E Minor* which is like insult to injury.

GENEVA. Is that why you're not practicing so much lately?

GERI. I'm not practicing at all. Ever again.

GENEVA. I can remember when you'd done a whole hour of scales by this time.

GERI. I thought I'd spare you.

GENEVA. You've always said you like this piano. Maybe we should trade. This one really belonged to your dad. Nobody ever plays it except you. If you like it better.

GERI. I don't want any of them. Leave it here.

GENEVA. My best memory of this room is bringing my breakfast in here at the crack of dawn and watching you play. Your dad conducting with a cigarette, counting out the time like a metranome.

GERI. A cigarette in one hand and a bottle of white wine in the other. You had to get to Laird before noon; his day was usually over about lunch time.

GENEVA. I like scales and exercises. I always have. The sound of industry maybe.

GERI. *(She glares mildly at Geneva.)* You're really pushing it. I suppose you love the sound of the sawmill too?

GENEVA. I loved the smell, not the noise.

GERI. If you really don't know I quit, I mean totally quit, then you're the only person in the whole wide world that doesn't know, because Julia's been like broadcasting it. She doesn't really care but it's thrilling conversation. I'm going to Paris and — I don't know, study cooking. Learn to do something people understand.

GENEVA.   *(She lets that pass.)* You seem to have recovered from your ordeal in the forest.

GERI.   It was my own fault. I have to get ready, some of the guys are going down to the river.

GENEVA.   Who was this "He" who caused you to faint? You were following another one of your Gray Eminences, weren't you? *(Geri doesn't answer.)* Geri, we can not have you harassing those men.

GERI.   I don't.

GENEVA.   You do too, Geri, and it's cruel. Also you can't know when one will be dangerous. Most of them are Army men, you realize. Trained at great expense to be homicidal. *(Beat.)* Who were you this time? Of them all, I think I like the anarchist exchange student from the Philippines trying to recruit a network of underground spies.

GERI.   Moles.

GENEVA.   How you get them to talk to you I'll never know. They won't to most people.

GERI.   Most people don't want them to.

GENEVA.   No, darling, that doesn't wash. I've said good morning several times and they've never even looked at me. You draw them out, get them talking about their lives, their war experiences that they clearly don't want to remember or they wouldn't be here. "Do you know my real father, his name is Ray Farrow, he has eyes like mine that don't match." I can't leave you alone for five minutes, you've got another one cornered. It isn't fair to Julia, it's an insult to Laird. I know you don't see it that way but your mother would shit a brick.

GERI.   She isn't my mother.

GENEVA.   Geri, you just exasperate the hell out of me. If Julia isn't your mother, Laird wasn't your father, I'm not your aunt, and you're a penniless little waif in some Dickensian orphanage. You have to take her as she comes and she'd shit a brick.

GERI.   I know. But she's so uptight she shits bricks at he least breach of etiquette. You could build a small village with the bricks mother's shat. It was bad enough when Laird was alive, pretending she didn't see he was like falling down drunk all the time, and I mean that took effort. But there's nothing of her in me at all. She's a fabulous mother —

GENEVA.   — She lets you do anything you damn well please.

GERI.   But it's not all that weird to wonder who I am, is it?

GENEVA.   You're very lucky. Most kids have no proof when they feel there must have been some tragic mix-up in the hospital, and these people they live with couldn't possibly be their real parents. You at least *know* you were adopted. That should be some consolation.

GERI.   It isn't.

GENEVA.   I don't know. I've watched you almost month by month develop into such a fine, talented young woman — you and Laird working so hard. You couldn't have been five, he knew already you were going to be better than he'd ever dreamed of being. By the time you were seven any fool could see it. I just feel I know you so well, I can't understand why you don't know yourself. You're just deliberately moving away from us. I expect any day now you'll start spouting Vietnamese and wearing a kimono.

GERI.   They don't wear kimonos. I know too much already and I don't know how I know it. A father over there literally *owns* his family. He could sell them if he wanted to.

GENEVA.   I wonder how much we could get for you.

GERI.   The whole family answers to the father; then the father answers to the mandarin; and the mandarin answers only to the emperor. I think I'm mandarin.

GENEVA.   Go for emperor.

GERI.   It's scary. It just slams into my head. I just suddenly know, or I hear or something: "Good conduct is learning to do exactly what your father did. Every movement a perfect repetition of his. Answer to your father before you." *(Beat.)* And I think, you know: (A) That's a crock. And (B) And we wonder why all the Vietnam kids are looking for their fathers? Wake up and learn something, God! And (C) Where the hell did that *come* from? And I appreciate that information a hell of a lot, but I have no idea what my father *did* before me, so like bugger off, okay? *(Less agitated.)* My ancestor's ashes have been scattered in a field over there, for a hundred generations. Three thousand years. So they're literally, physically nourishing their descendants. Or this voice says, "If you do everything correctly," which is exactly as it's always done, I suppose, to the last detail, "then you'll be content. Fields will prosper, the weather will be fair, and calm will prevail.

GENEVA.   I don't understand those rice cultures.

GERI.   Obviously not. You're selling everything your ancestors have done down the toilet.

GENEVA.   The hell I am. We've spent a fortune fighting those S.O.B.s.

GERI.   Oh, I don't care! Do what you have to do. Who am *I*? How do I do what my father has done before me? What? Should I go to war and come back and drink myself under the table every night like Laird? Or, being a woman, I'll go around like Julia, dragging her sable from one Board Meeting to another, dropping a hundred thousand dollars on every charity that licks her ass.

GENEVA.   Geri, please! Every charity that *kisses* her ass, not licks her ass.

GERI.   *(Pause.)* I like the sound, though. "And calm will prevail."

GENEVA.   *(Beat.)* It has a definite ring.

GERI.   I was talking to the man Buzz Warren ran over in the alley.

GENEVA.   Oh, good lord. John Doe? No wonder you fainted.

GERI.   He has a name.

GENEVA.   Well, if he does, he doesn't know it. Elaine said he didn't even know his own name. Mumbled and jumbled and left before they'd set his foot properly.

GERI.   He talks fine. He's just very private.

GENEVA.   That's clear, I think.

GERI.   And a thief, but I don't blame him.

GENEVA.   How much money did you give him?

GERI.   Give? I didn't give —

GENEVA.   What were you carrying?

GERI.   Six hundred.

GENEVA.   Oh, good Lord. If you weren't going home tomorrow, I think I'd send you back anyway.

GERI.   I wasn't planning on fainting. It must have been the sun. I was so eager to flaunt my powers I banished every trace of cloud cover. It got hot as the devil in there.

GENEVA.   That was you? I had to turn on the air conditioning. Julia is going to have to talk to you about managing your money.

GERI.   I know from her example: Unless they name a building after you, never, under any circumstances, let go of a single nickel.

GENEVA.   I don't know. For entertainment we used to go roller-skating. For mental stimulation we'd read a good book. It was always a *good* book, we never said I'd like to curl up with just a book. He is absolutely the last one you talk to.

GERI.   Okay.

GENEVA.   I mean it.

GERI.   Okay!

GENEVA.   What's his name?

GERI.   He didn't tell me. He blew up bridges. It destroyed his hearing I think.

GENEVA.   That'd be the least of his afflictions. They must have ear plugs. Besides, they can't just stand there and watch it blow up.

GERI.   He's growing pot out in your woods.

GENEVA.   He didn't happen to give you any, for your trouble? Some very good ganja has come out of those woods. I've come across whole farms of it. I was walking along, carrying David, he couldn't have been more than two, and suddenly came out into this clearing with a little house and a very big man with an even bigger dog and a shotgun. I just said, "Oh, I'm terribly sorry, we were looking for the river," turned around and walked straight home, thank you. Expecting to be shot in the back of the head with every step. That's another reason I don't want you wandering around out there. Also they don't belong to us anymore. We don't belong there. God, it kills me to say that. I don't have a memory, there's not a single family story that isn't connected to those trees. If I'm not a lumberjack, I don't know what the hell I am.

GERI.   They're never going to finalize the sale.

GENEVA.   Hostile take over! There was no goddamn sale, we weren't *for* sale!

GERI.   Yeah, but you know lawyers, they've dragged it out for three years, they'll drag it out for centuries.

GENEVA.   All done. This morning. While you were getting your beauty sleep. I wasn't going to tell you. We caved in. Or bit the bullet.

GERI.   Oh, no.

GENEVA.   Well, it was over.

GERI.   I mean Julia said not to bring it up because you couldn't possibly win, but I'm so used to you fighting them.

GENEVA.   No more. And don't get used to things. We signed our names with a flourish on a hundred lines. I've never been so angry in my life. Or left so impotent. Barney chain smoking. He kept saying, I know you hate the smoke, but I can't not smoke right now. If he's buying something or selling something. He thinks he's let my family down. They let themselves down, going public in the first place. But who'd ever heard of a take over back then. Everybody said it'll still just be a little family concern. Sure. Some bastard offers twice what the stock is going for, all your "buddies" on the board fall all over themselves to be first in line. You'd think they'd be terribly disappointed in themselves to discover they have their price. Hell, no. They're not lumber men anymore, they're moguls.

GERI.   You'll be pretty well compensated, though.

GENEVA.   The point isn't the money. The point is some no-name gasket company from Pittsburgh, and some C.E.O. from Houston can take over a hundred-twenty-year-old family company and just trash it.

GERI.   How much will you get, though?

GENEVA.   Oh — It's been reported in every paper in the country. We have twenty percent of the holding; they're getting 700 million, $50 a share.

GERI.   A hundred forty million.

GENEVA.   Hardly. Taxes, love. To death. Less than half that.

GERI.   A lousy 60 million dollars.

GENEVA. What the hell are we going to do with money like that? We're not your mother and her jet-set crowd. *(Beat.)* And it isn't enough. I could say I cared for a hundred thousand acres of redwood forest. The oldest living thing. I was on a goddamned float in the parade when I was 10, dressed like a shepherdess, with hundreds of little knee-high trees around me. Sheperdess of the Redwoods. *(Geri is smiling.)* Well, damnit, I *felt* like the Shepherdess of the Redwoods. I don't expect a damn wood nymph to understand, but I did! We've harvested them so conscientiously; everyone in town thought we were too conservative. Even the goddamned Sierra Club approved! We were cutting trees my great great grandfather planted. These guys have borrowed all that money. You can't manage a forest from debt. They're just going to mow them down. Environmentalists are gonna have a field day, honey. The fertilizer is gonna hit the ol' fan.
GERI. Maybe the new manager won't be that bad.
GENEVA. The man is from Texas, there's not a tree in the state. Prosperity for 10 years, then this burg will be a ghost town.
GERI. You knew it was coming though; you always said you couldn't win. You haven't set foot in the forest since that company made their first bid.
GENEVA. Well, not my problem anymore. Not Barney's problem. To hell with all of them. But I'm angry. It's very easy to be a success in this world, Geri. All you have to do is change your goals.
GERI. Maybe it was just time to retire.
GENEVA. Geri, nobody likes you when you take this devil's advocate position. It's not about the money. If all I wanted was to be rich I could be rich. You get a job at a security exchange house, practice insider trading, make eight hundred million dollars, get caught, get convicted, pay five hundred million in fines and taxes, go to jail for 5 years, get out in 2. I know very few men of 30 who wouldn't spend 2 years in jail for three hundred million dollars. *(Beat.)* And I don't like the way you throw around phrases like "It's time for you to retire." These bastards are cutting me off at the roots. Forc-

ing me out of my own damn house.

GERI.   You wouldn't leave Arcata.

GENEVA.   Go look out on the front lawn. The sign went up this morning.

GERI.   No.

GENEVA.   Damned if I'm going to be the brunt of all the local indignation when the boom busts. The real estate Dough Boy was literally salivating. He said, we'll just keep this listing between ourselves. I said, No way! I want the whole state of California to know I'm out of here. Put up a sign with the finger on it.

GERI.   You can't leave here.

GENEVA.   You just watch me.

GERI.   I spend the whole year waiting to come up here.

GENEVA.   You'll like Key Biscayne just as well.

GERI.   I hate Key Biscayne. You hate Key Biscayne.

GENEVA.   Well, tough. Barney loves it. He thinks he's a deep sea fisherman. He said, if you really want it, we can pick up some land south of Eureka, but no more. No more logging. It really is going to be nice to sit on my butt and not panic every time I smell smoke; looking at the sky to see if it's ever going to rain. Wondering if it would look too showy for this town if I got a new car or a chauffeur. We'll be somewhere where everyone has money and nobody has an attack if you spend it. And I don't care how that sounds. We've done a good job.

GERI.   If I can't come here — I'll never find him. This one is really not like the others.

GENEVA.   *(Deliberately changing the subject.)* You think you could manage breakfast before you hit the river?

GERI.   No.

GENEVA.   Geri, no! You are not to go looking for that man. Or any of them. They don't want it, it isn't fair to them. You're just setting yourself up for another disappointment.

GERI.   How do you know he doesn't want it?

GENEVA.   Well, does he present an invitation to society in your view?

GERI.   Who knows? Maybe he just doesn't know —

GENEVA.   No, darling, thank you, but my own brother came back from that war totally whacko. Laird never drank before. If you're going to visit us we have to be responsible for you. You're not just any old curious tomboy; you're rather special, you know. You're one of the best young pianists this country has ever produced.

GERI.   My decision on that is absolutely final.

GENEVA.   If you have talent like that, you have no choice but to practice it.

GERI.   That's The Protestant Ethic, it has nothing to do with Asians.

GENEVA.   Oh, you drive me crazy sometimes.

GERI.   And I'd as soon give up the magic while I'm at it. Where has it got me except for being the adopted daughter of a wealthy family that lets me do anything I please.

GENEVA.   It isn't funny. Your mother really would just let you throw it all away. I could just shake her. I can't wait to tell her you've decided to become a cook.

GERI.   As long as it doesn't inconvenience her summers in Italy. My schedule was getting too complicated for her, anyway.

GENEVA.   She says you haven't practiced in two months. You haven't touched the piano since you've been here. I've listened every morning, waiting to hear you play.

GERI.   Don't hold your breath.

GENEVA.   Did you cancel your recital in Chicago?

GERI.   Yes. And the recording session. All of it. I'm not joking.

GENEVA.   Are you tired?

GERI.   I'm not tired, damnit, I've just had it. And I don't think it's at all unusual or sick or egocentric to want to be a normal human being or to be liked or appreciated in something.

GENEVA.   You're appreciated. Enormously.

GERI.   I'm not appreciated, I'm "Special." Every time I walk out on stage. "Oh, isn't she tiny, isn't she just adorable. She's a Vietnam War bastard, you know. She has no idea who her mother and father are. Aren't we lucky one of them turned out to be special." Sony Classical wanted to call my album "America's Children"! And I don't see why having a talent or a gift, even if it's for just sticking at something and sitting on my rear end and practicing, which is all I have, anyway — I have a tolerance for repeating scales and exercises ad nauseam; apparently I enjoy my fingers swelling up and having my nails bleed and walking around with Band-Aids on all my fingers — and I don't know why someone with whatever that is, that gift or curse or liability or handicap (it's like you can only be given something, even of whatever questionable value, if you're simultaneously eviscerated of everything anyone holds as worthy or admirable or real or worthwhile) I don't know why someone like that has to be treated like a freak of nature, like they have seven arms like Shiva or however many he has, and tiptoed around like they're sick or maimed or consumptive or an invalid or special in some way. I don't want to be special. *(Pause.)*

GENEVA.   You're special, Geri. *(Pause.)*

GERI.   I know I am. *(She walks out of the room.)*

GENEVA.   Honey.

GERI.   *(Off.)* I've got to change. I'm going down to the river.

GENEVA.   Let me drive you.

GERI.   *(Off.)* No. *(We hear the front door slam. After a moment, behind Geneva, Lyman appears in the open doorway. She hears him and turns, seeing him.)*

GENEVA.   *(Starting.)* Oh. Dear God in heaven.

LYMAN.   You Mrs. Smith?

GENEVA.   *(After she collects herself.)* I have the feeling that my niece was possibly rude to you yesterday and owes you an apology. She isn't in just now, but maybe you'll accept mine. *(Beat.)* And I believe that you inadvertently took something that belongs to her.

LYMAN.   Your husband Dr. Smith?

GENEVA.   No.

LYMAN.   He teach arithmetic at the school?

GENEVA.   My husband? My husband drives down to the mill once a month and walks through with a great grin on his face saying, "Lookin' good, boys, lookin' good, boys," gets back in his car, drives home, comes in the house and says, "It's lookin' good, Genny." *(Beat.)* He also pays the bills and signs the paychecks. *(Beat.)* I was just getting ready to go out. So I'm afraid I'm going to have to ask you to leave.

LYMAN.   *(Flashing Geri's photograph from her wallet.)* You know this girl?

GENEVA.   That's my niece. *(She reaches for the wallet; he doesn't offer it.)*

LYMAN.   What's her name?

GENEVA.   Geri Riordan. It's probably in there.

LYMAN.   Her name's not Geraldine Lon?

GENEVA.   She has a phony driver's license with the name Geraldine Lon on it, that says she's of age. I'm not supposed to know that. She had them put down Lon as a joke. *(Beat.)* I guess you had to be there. We call her Geri. But her name is Riordan, not Lon.

LYMAN.   *(He flashes another picture.)* That her mother?

GENEVA.   Geri, what the hell have you been doing. That's a photograph of some Chinese film star, Geri doesn't even know her name. No, that's not Geri's mother. She has a rather eccentric sense of humor.

LYMAN.   *(Holds up another photo.)* That her foster dad?

GENEVA.   Yes.

LYMAN.   He drink himself to death?

GENEVA.   Laird was my brother. He came home from the war very troubled. You might understand that. Or not.

LYMAN.   She live here?

GENEVA.   No. Now, if you'll —

LYMAN.   She said she was staying with Dr. Smith.

GENEVA.   I don't know any damn Dr. Smith. I don't know Mrs. Smith. Off the top of my head I don't think I've ever known a Smith in my life.

LYMAN.   *(He hands her the wallet.)* Count the money.

GENEVA.   It's fine, I'm sure.

LYMAN.   Count the money!

GENEVA.   I'm sure it's — Well, why not? 1, 2, 3, 4.   600 dollars. It's remarkable to get it back with that much cash.

LYMAN.   Where would I break a 50 dollar bill?

GENEVA.   Mr. Doe. Let's just not thrash around that bush, okay? There are 10 bars in Arcata that would happily serve a baboon with the price of a drink. If you're hinting for a reward, it's the most ludicrous suggestion I've ever heard.

LYMAN.   You let her follow people around town? Let her walk around town with money like that?

GENEVA.   Thank you for returning this. She'll be very glad to have it back. Now, if you'll —

LYMAN.   She ever tell the truth? *(Geneva is preparing to close the door in his face.)* She telling the truth when she said her dad was to Vietnam? *(She is stopped dead a moment. She looks over his shoulder to the yard.)*

GENEVA.   *(Not a reprimand.)* Is that your dog out in my dahlias? *(Beat.)* What's her name?

LYMAN.   I call her "Bitch."

GENEVA.   I have a friend who would say "Droll." I'm sure it's all in the tone of voice. Mr. ... I don't know what my niece has been telling you. She's visiting here for the month. She does every June, since she was 12. She goes home tomorrow. She has a habit of talking to strangers.

LYMAN.   She told me she'd never seen the trees before.

GENEVA.   Well, as I said, she's here every summer.

LYMAN.   She said her dad's name was Ray Farrow.

GENEVA.   She's — No. No, I'm not going to go into this with you. I'll apologize for any inconvenience Geri's caused you. I'm ... sorry about your hearing, you cope very well.

LYMAN.   I hear okay.

GENEVA.   I understood you blew up bridges in the war.

LYMAN.   Yeah.

GENEVA.   And it impaired your hearing.

LYMAN.   You wear plugs.

GENEVA.   I see. *(He hands her a set of dog tags.)*

LYMAN.   I put these on the dog, I don't wear them anymore.

GENEVA.   You keep your dog tags on your dog. That's very ... *(She reads the tag.)* This is you? "Lyman Fellers"? *(He gives no indication. After a moment.)* Come in, have a seat.

LYMAN.   I'm fine. *(He remains standing in the doorway. Geneva walks around the room a moment, landing at the bar.)*

GENEVA.   You didn't tell Geri your name.

LYMAN.   That doesn't matter.

GENEVA.   It'll matter a hell of a lot to her. What did she tell you?

LYMAN.   She's looking for her dad.

GENEVA.   Yes, well, all of them are, aren't they? Half the people in America are looking for their fathers. You see it on television all the time. Hopelessly arrogant young men and women claiming their right to know their biological parents at whatever cost to everyone else. Julia always said you'd turn up one day. They spotted you in Hopland a few years back, gave us a general description of who you were, she nearly died. That's the only reason Geri comes here. She's been systematically interviewing all of you ... *(She gropes for a word to call them, then goes on.)* in the whole Great Northwest Territory. Every June since she was 12. *(Pause. She looks at the dog tags, rubbing one between her thumb and finger.)* I'm not ready for this. You should know that Geri's mother gave her up for adoption the moment she set foot in this country. Geri was less than a month old. The only information we've had about you is what she told us: The father was a service man named "Farrow." With one brown — *(Looking him directly in the face, she breaks off.)* Oh, dear god — well, I knew that, didn't I? *(She musters on through.)* Who had one blue eye and one brown and a tattoo of an eagle somewhere on his ... I'll take that on faith. She gave her name as "Lily Lon." Subsequent investigations proved that information erron — why am I talking like that? The name Lily Lon was a phony. I always thought your description was so far-fetched that you were a figment too. My brother Laird just laughed. Geri bought it, of course. I probably would too, if that was the only thing I had. *(Beat.)* Geri has been well loved and cared for. As it happens she's developed into one of the most promising pianists to come down the pike in a hell of a long time. She had her first recital 5 years ago. She's been all over the country. And England and France. Japan. She just completed a tour with the St. Louis Symphony. She's exhausted; she's trying to do too much. She finished school, she was going to go to Juilliard next year on a full scholarship. Right now she's off music; I don't know what the hell she wants.

LYMAN. She's not looking at schools?

GENEVA. What? No. The only thing she cares about is "finding herself." I thought we finished with that in the sixties. This is tragic. Excuse me, but your timing couldn't be worse.

LYMAN. She knows plants?

GENEVA. What?

LYMAN. She studies plants?

GENEVA. No. I don't know what she's told you. You shouldn't —

LYMAN. She said her dad grew up in a small town.

GENEVA. We weren't told that. She guesses as much as she knows.

LYMAN. She said her mother owned a flower shop in Nam.

GENEVA. Her mother was a child, 14 or 15 as I'm sure you well know. She barely knew English. My brother and his wife gave the girl 25 thousand dollars for Geri. The adoption was totally legal but definitely not through the usual channels; the usual channels are too slow for Julia.

LYMAN. Shrewd cookie. Drives a stiff bargain.

GENEVA. You better believe it. I imagine if the father showed up and agreed to waive all claims, and not attempt to see Geri again, he could expect to get at least that much. *(Beat.)* Probably a good deal more. I'll give you a number you can call.

LYMAN. He built stuff?

GENEVA. I'm sorry?

LYMAN. Geri said her dad was studying to be a builder.

GENEVA. We don't know that. We've never known anything about what her natural father did. *(Pause.)*

LYMAN. I wanted to build things.

GENEVA. Oh, my god. *(She is having a mild but sincere attack of empathy.)* Mr. Fellers. I don't know what to say. I'll just kill her, I really will. I'll just take a ballbat — *(Beat.)* What do you want? Just tell me what it is you want.

LYMAN. You tell your niece not to talk to strangers. *(He turns and leaves. The lights fade to black.)*

SCENE THREE

A coffee house in Arcata. Geri sits at a table with a cup of coffee, studying a map. After a moment Geneva enters. She walks to the table and drops Geri's wallet on it.

GENEVA.   Your putative father and Bitch dropped by the house. Get your stuff together and let's get out of here. This coffee house refuses to serve me. I sat here once for half an hour, nobody gave me the time of day.

GERI.   They don't have table service, you have to go to the counter.

GENEVA.   I'm too old to live in a college town.

GERI.   What did he tell you?

GENEVA.   She showed me his dog tags, probably the only identification he has. Right now you've got that man so confused I don't think he knows if he's your father or not.

GERI.   I think he is. His name is Ray Farrow isn't it?

GENEVA.   No, and if I told you it was nothing like that would you still try to see him?

GERI.   Are you crazy?

GENEVA.   That's what I thought. *(She sits.)* You're not going to talk to that man again unless I'm there.

GERI.   It's a deal.

GENEVA.   I've driven up and down every street and alley in Arcata trying to find him. Half way to Ferndale, up 101 damn near to Larrupin'. I've put 90 miles on the car. Finally I saw one of your swimming buddies in town.

GERI.   I didn't go swimming.

GENEVA.   I realize that. I asked the woman at the shelter if she'd seen John Doe, she said, "Oh, Geri was just asking about him." You didn't find him either?

GERI.   No. I think he's gone back to he woods.

GENEVA.   Oh, god. I can't do it. I can't go back in there. *(Beat.)*

GERI.   Will you tell me his name?

GENEVA.   His name is Lyman Fellers.

GERI.   Lyman Fellers? I don't care. He has an eagle tattooed on his arm.

GENEVA.   Ten thousand soldiers must have that tattoo.

GERI.   I know they do.

GENEVA.   You told him about that, too?

GERI.   No.

GENEVA.   Well, it doesn't matter. I did. What is that, a map?

GERI.   *(Showing Geneva the map.)* I think we were here. The closest place you could drive to is over here.

GENEVA.   That's the other side of fern valley. I can hardly tramp through the woods dressed like this.

GERI.   You know the way better than I do. It's not that far. If you go by the house you'll want to change clothes, then you'll want to leave a note for Uncle Barney. It'll be dark. I'm going. You can take me or not. *(Geri reaches for the map.)*

GENEVA.   *(Taking the map from Geri.)* Geri, I'm exhausted. Is there sugar in this?

GERI.   No. *(Geneva puts three sugars in the coffee, stirs it and drinks it down.)*

GENEVA.   Child, child, child. Why you want your father to be someone like that is ...

GERI.   I don't want it or not, I just think it's true. Don't you feel it? That kind of completely inhuman, asocial behavior. Wandering around by myself. Shut up in a 2 by 4 rehearsal room 8 hours a day. Having so few friends. Not believing anything anyone says to me.

GENEVA.   Well, whose fault is that?

GERI.   Maybe it's his.

GENEVA.   And no, I don't feel it. You're an artist. Artists are crazy.

GERI.   No more.

GENEVA.   Geri, he's not well. He's been deeply — he's a — I'm trying to think of a way to talk about the man without sounding prejudicial or maudlin or — Well, I can't. But that's a fine reason to want to know your parents: having someone to blame your idiosyncrasies on. You actually followed him through the woods?

GERI.   I thought maybe he'd, I don't know, sing to himself, or whistle or something.

GENEVA.   Oh, god. If this doesn't kill me, Julia will. Did he? Whistle?

GERI.   He knew I was following him.

GENEVA.   I whistle. I've even been known to sing to myself. Julia played the piano. David thinks he can play the guitar —

GERI.   — Julia's never touched that piano in her life. It was Laird's piano.

GENEVA.   You were brought up in household that appreciates music. Some things are *learned*, Geri.

GERI.   Some things are not. (*They stand. The table goes away. The lights come up on the woods; they walk into it, calling.*) Hello! Hello! What'd he tell you his name was?

GENEVA.   Lyman Fellers.

GERI.   (*Calling.*) Mr. Fellers! Mr. Fellers! (*She waits, listening.*) Well, there's no sign of him at all.

GENEVA.   Is this where he was?

GERI.   Yes.

GENEVA.   Oh god. This is killing me. It's just ripping my heart out.

GERI.   I wasn't thinking, did we walk too fast?

GENEVA.   You unfeeling little wretch. I'm as strong as a horse. Some of my friends say I look almost exactly like a horse. I don't care if you *don't* ever get winded, I can run you around these woods ten times. They're not mine anymore, Geri. I'm seeing them. I'm walking through them, it's just ripping my heart out.

GERI.   I know. (*She is looking through the wallet.*) He's been through every thing in here. All the pictures have been taken out and put back the opposite of the way they were.

GENEVA.   Maybe he's dyslexic on top of everything else.

GERI.   He's even been at the secret compartment.

GENEVA.   What have you got in there?

GERI.   Nothing. Every wallet has one, what's the point? My library card, the note from Tom.

GENEVA.   What did he mean, "Dear Geri, Thanks for the heart attack. Love, Tom?"

GERI.   I knew it. I hate it when you snoop through my

things. Tom told me he didn't want to take Phys. Ed. I told him to go to the nurse and complain of a pain in his chest and she'd give him an E.K.G. that said he had a fluttery heart and they'd excuse him from Phys. Ed.

GENEVA.   Does he have a fluttery heart?

GERI.   Of course not. I only gave him a fluttery heart while he was having the E.K.G.

GENEVA.   Does any of that sorcery — well, not that, genie-ness ever get you anything worth while? Like learning a new mazurka or doubling your considerable fortune?

GERI.   No. I think it's supposed to guide me; it's not doing a very good job. *(There is the sound of a twig breaking off in the woods. They freeze, listening. Geri calls lightly.)* I know you'll come out when you want to.

GENEVA.   God, this is a beautiful spot. Dad used to carry me through here on his shoulders. I'm just being bombarded with memories of — are you doing some *(Gestures.)* fairy dust number on me or something? I'm feeling very weird here.

GERI.   I have no idea what you're talking about.

GENEVA.   You should think about what you're going to say if he shows up. The man's obviously been mulling over every stupid thing you told him. Doctor Smith? Geraldine Lon? Your mother sold flowers?

GERI.   She did.

GENEVA.   How do you know she — well, I won't ask. You'll only say "I never know."

GERI.   I don't.

GENEVA.   God, the smell out here! They're going to cut this whole place flat.

GERI.   *(Calling.)* Mr. Fellers! *(To Geneva.)* What if he isn't? That'd be worse than if he was. He said he never fraternized. That's hardly something you'd forget. I mean you'd expect the man to remember if he'd got laid.

GENEVA.   Geri.

GERI.   And his name is wrong.

GENEVA.   Lyman Fellers? Oh, we've known that name for years.

GERI.   We have?

GENEVA. Your people, the agency, whatever they're called, who hunt down children's parents, must have told you about the man in Hopland.

GERI. It had to be Ray Farrow, how many people look like that? But he didn't have any identification.

GENEVA. Julia and Laird just saw that his name got lost in the report.

GERI. What was his name then?

GENEVA. The man in Hopland? Your buddy. Lyman Fellers.

GERI. Well that's wrong. Unless I've been lied to all my life.

GENEVA. Wouldn't that be poetic justice. No, they've always told you what your natural mother said. That's the point. (*She sits on a stump or rock, makes herself comfortable.*) Have you met Suki Sato? Secretary of the Village Improvement Association of Key Biscayne.

GERI. No.

GENEVA. Wonderful Japanese lady. Used to answer the phone "Bearage Employment." We adored her. One Christmas — they have this Yuletide lobster pig-out dance. A kind of Tex-Mex luau. David and Sharon were supposed to go but they were having their biennial brabble. I was on the phone with Suki. I said I thought it was pretty useless to expect David and Sharon, or at least to expect them to come together. And she sighed and said, "Aw, Rubber Squirrel." We adored her. I had no idea what she was talking about half the time. Well, you know me I never listen to anyone really. I just said, fine, whatever. Naturally I was driving. In the middle of the Richenbacher Causeway, I started laughing so hard I had to pull over or get us killed. Barney. I explained it to him. Maybe you had to be there. He still doesn't get it.

GERI. Get what?

GENEVA. They were having a "Rubber Squirrel," Geri. (*Beat.*) "Lover's quarrel." (*Pause. Geri gives no indication of understanding.*)

GERI. It's an area of humor I've never really responded to.

GENEVA. I swear to God your brain has gone to pulp. You're as dumb as lumber sometimes. Geri. "Lover's quarrel," "Rubber squirrel." "Lyman Fellers." … "Raymond Farrow" —

43

GERI. — Raymond Farrow. Oh, but that's really reaching.

GENEVA. Nevertheless, that's what Mr. Fellers has been thinking. I imagine he heard his name pronounced just that way over there. When Julia heard it it scared her spitless.

GERI. I'd guess. What? Scandal, blackmail, bribery.

GENEVA. It isn't a joke. No, she was afraid of losing you. That's why she's so damned overprotective. You're the only thing she has she couldn't bear to lose.

GERI. *(Unmoved.)* That has to be underscored with like Mendelssohn or something. *(Beat.)* Lyman Fellers. He really may be my father then.

GENEVA. I got the impression he's not going to admit it. And if that's his game, fine. You're going to find out if he's willing to tell you anything about the circumstances of your birth, apologize for messing his mind up, and we're getting out of here. I don't want you hassling him.

GERI. If he's my father I'm not going to just leave him here.

GENEVA. If that's what he wants, you certainly will.

GERI. It isn't what he wants.

GENEVA. You don't know that.

GERI. I do too.

GENEVA. You do not.

GERI. I do too.

GENEVA. Oh, Lordy. Your mother will kill me. She'd have you as far away from "Raymond Farrow" as she could get you. Rome. *(Beat.)* You may as well know that I told him it'd probably be worth a lot of money if he disappeared.

GERI. *What?*

GENEVA. Well, it would be.

GERI. Do you have any idea what this means to me?

GENEVA. I was thinking what it means to us.

GERI. What did he say?

GENEVA. I was so circumspect and he was so confused, I don't think he even knew I was trying to buy him off. Watch him come here now and say, yes, I'm your father, what's it worth?

GERI. At least I'd know.

GENEVA. Oh, fine. And how are you going to follow in your father's footsteps in the time-honored tradition of the Vietnamese? Bang yourself over the head with a board and walk around La Jolla like a bag lady? (*Beat.*) You're already weird. (*She looks down at Geri who seems lost in thought, her energy gone.*)

GERI. He wanted to be an engineer.

GENEVA. I know, he told me. Oh, Lordy. What in the deep rocky hell is life supposed to be about? If you want to be an engineer, you think you have to be an engineer, then be a damn engineer. (*Beat.*) You're so strong and you have such energy, and such superhuman talent, I forget how young you are, chicken. Why don't we go on home? Huh? It's going to start getting cold, then it'll be dark. Then it'll really get cold. (*She is looking around her at the trees.*) God, it's so quiet here. I don't think I can let them go, Geri. That stupid gasket company is going to need cash so badly ... I think they'd jump at the chance to sell some of it off. I could buy back this section. down to the fern valley.

GERI. "Shepherdess of the Redwoods" — ?

GENEVA. — I knew I'd regret telling you that.

GERI. You don't have the sawmill anymore, you couldn't work it.

GENEVA. I'd have the trees.

GERI. Could you afford to just have them?

GENEVA. Well, I'm not saying I wouldn't keep something to live on.

GERI. Uncle Barney would hate it.

GENEVA. He really would. He loves Key Biscayne. He sees us retiring as The Old Man and the Sea and His Old Lady. Never get married, Geri, your whole life is a compromise. (*A pause. A dog barks, not too far off. Geri and Geneva look up. Lyman is standing, watching them. He walks toward them, looking at Geri all the while. After a moment he addresses Geri.*)

LYMAN. I hunt. I fish sometimes. I don't cat garbage. There's a coffee shop place called Wildflower, the lady leaves rolls out sometimes.

GENEVA. They use almost no butter in their cooking.

GERI.   Aunt Geneva.

GENEVA.   Well, excuse me for living. Barney and I eat there all the time.

LYMAN.   I built a shelter place where I sleep 'cause of the rain. It's not bad.

GERI.   Good.

LYMAN.   I'm fine.

GERI.   Good.

LYMAN.   Were you really dead?

GERI.   Yes.

LYMAN.   You didn't see the White Light?

GERI.   No.

LYMAN.   What did you see?

GERI.   Nothing.

LYMAN.   You have a plastic hip?

GENEVA.   Geri, what have you been telling him? She was on the operating table for 7 hours.

GERI.   I came close to having to have one. And a steel rod in my spine, too. They would have if it hadn't been for my heart. Really.

LYMAN.   Yeah.

GERI.   The doctor told me. You can ask him.

LYMAN.   You been all over. You probably already seen a maze.

GERI.   Hampton Court in Middlesex. It works, I tried it.

LYMAN.   Your mother sell flowers in Saigon?

GENEVA.   We don't know what she did or where she came from.

GERI.   She did.

LYMAN.   I grew up in Akron.

GENEVA.   Where?

LYMAN.   Akron. Ohio, ma'am. My dad had a garage I worked in. I enlisted senior year out of high school. I didn't have no girlfriends; they never said yes or no. Wasn't any square to drive around; we was all jet heads. Drag raced. Muscle cars; ride around alone, act like fools. I had a Mustang. Boss 302. Za good car.

GERI.   I'll bet you were good. That sounds patronizing. I

46

don't mean it that way. I meant I'll bet you were good.

LYMAN.   I won some.

GENEVA.   Mr. Fellers, Geri has something she'd like to say to you. *(Pause. Geri studies him a moment.)*

GERI.   Why do you live the way you do?

LYMAN.   I'm fine. *(Pause.)* I eat okay, I sleep okay. I don't need nothing else. It don't matter what other people do — that's them, I'm me. I'm okay.

GERI.   No. You're not okay at all. *(A pause.)*

LYMAN.   *(To Geri.)* I held you in my arms. You wasn't any bigger than that. Not a week old. *(A stunned silence. Geri looks to Geneva then back to Lyman.)* Every village over in Nam got a post in the middle for the spirits. They got genies all over, damn near every village. They do weird stuff. Your mother probably was one, I didn't know.

GERI.   What was her name?

LYMAN.   I heard it. I can't remember that language. She wasn't a kid like you said; she was older than us, she was 25 – 30. She didn't come over here like you said. She stayed there.

GERI.   She's still there?

LYMAN.   Probably. *(To Geneva.)* You should have told her.

GENEVA.   Geri's mother was described to us as a child 14 or 15. Geri's been told everything we know.

LYMAN.   I bet I knew the girl your mother gave you to to bring you over here. She was just some kid, wanted to come to the states. Probably didn't give her right name. She got 25 thousand dollars? She did okay. *(Beat.)* I didn't sign no papers to bring her over here. They shouldn't of used my name.

GERI.   Are you my father?

LYMAN.   No ma'am, I'm not.

GERI.   But you know who he is.

LYMAN.   They shouldn't of used my name without telling me.

GERI.   Why did they then?

LYMAN.   'Cause of the eyes probably. Made them think of it. I don't think you inherit eyes like a husky dog, you're just born with them. Freak of nature. Never did me any good. I don't want to tell you people things you shouldn't know. It don't matter.

GERI. It matters, damnit. It matters a hell of a lot to me.

LYMAN. What do you care where you came from? You know who you are. You're who you are. You're okay. You're almost grown up.

GERI. I will turn you into a green jumping toad. I'm not joking.

GENEVA. Geri, don't say that. Actually I don't think she could. That stuff she does has to be beneficial to someone. Some of the kids wanted to get out of a history class early, Geri caused a total solar eclipse. Only the kids in her room saw it. Caused an enormous confusion. The teacher wouldn't even talk about it after a while. Am I to understand that you knew Geri's parents in Vietnam?

LYMAN. Yes, ma'am. I didn't think so at first, except for the flower shop.

GENEVA. And you're not claiming to be her father.

LYMAN. No, ma'am.

GENEVA. But you think you know who he is.

LYMAN. Some things I can remember, some things I don't. Yeah, I know.

GENEVA. You can pick one child out of 40 thousand orphans and recognize her sixteen years later.

LYMAN. *(To Geri.)* What did you say the odds was?

GERI. 1 in 10 million. Same as the Lottery.

LYMAN. They was worried about your eyes.

GERI. They're fine.

LYMAN. I tried to tell 'em. They was hysterical about it. Nobody knew your mother was going to have a kid. She wasn't much bigger than you, but you couldn't tell. She was a stylish woman. She was like the women over there are, the ones with a little money, they're like you think French women would be. She got pregnant, she started wearing those big coats they wear and all. *(Beat.)* Your dad wanted you and him and your mother to live over there, but they wouldn't let him stay. He was all torn up. He felt things too much, got depressed all the time. Lay around, mope around, saddest man

I ever knew. *(Pause. He is reluctant to go on.)* He loved you a lot. He was real proud. Some of us was in town, he had us come in the back of the flower shop and showed you to us. We passed you around. He was real proud. He couldn't bring her over here, he already had a wife in the states. But he had to keep you.

GERI. Why didn't he?

LYMAN. He did. *(Pause.)* He was okay. He had the strongest hands of any man I ever shook hands with. He was gonna fix it up with the adoption people. So I guess that's what he did.

GENEVA. Oh, dear sweet God.

LYMAN. Looks like he'd of told you.

GENEVA. No. He could never have hurt Julia. He couldn't have told any of us, she'd have guessed.

GERI. Laird?

GENEVA. Of course.

GERI. You knew?

GENEVA. No. *(To Lyman.)* He was in love with her. With Geri's mother, wasn't he?

LYMAN. Yes, ma'am.

GENEVA. And he was fine till he found out he couldn't stay there. We've never known why he changed — he became so ...

GERI. You're right, Lyman, he was the saddest man I've ever known.

LYMAN. You didn't want to know, maybe you'll learn to leave people alone. He was okay, but he had no business using my name.

GERI. You don't remember my mother's name?

LYMAN. No, ma'am.

GERI. *(Angry.)* She couldn't keep me there? What, was she afraid she'd lose the business?

LYMAN. You want people to be perfect? People ain't perfect.

GERI. Laird. Good Lord. And I thought I was joking when I said to follow in my father's footsteps I had to mope and pine and drink myself to death. Not a very promising path

49

he's laid out for me to follow.

GENEVA.   You didn't really know him; he wasn't like that before the war.

LYMAN.   He didn't drink. Over there he didn't drink.

GERI.   What did he do?

LYMAN.   He played the piano. *(A pause.)*

GERI.   He was a hell of a teacher.

GENEVA.   Are you all right?

GERI.   I told you my mother had a flower shop.

GENEVA.   I could go with you. To Vietnam. We could think of something. I mean we could go to, I don't know, you could tour Japan again as much as you don't like it, and we could go from there.

GERI.   Vietnam is hardly a place you drop in on.

GENEVA.   You've never played Sydney. I have friends in Australia. You've needed someone to manage you since Laird ... God knows I have the time.

GERI.   He played the piano.

GENEVA.   Julia gets no kick out of touring with you and I love it, so —

GERI.   Julia!

GENEVA.   Oh, good Lord, Julia! She'll never be able to take it, Geri.

GERI.   We can't tell her. Lyman! *(Both at once they notice he is no longer there.)* Lyman!

GENEVA.   Mr. Fellers! Mr. Fellers! *(Geri runs off and back and off the other way looking for him.)*

GERI.   Where the hell did he go? Ly-man!

GENEVA.   Mr. Fellers! Geri, get him back.

GERI.   I can't. It won't work unless he's looking in my eyes.

GENEVA.   Well, try.

GERI.   *(Calling at the top of her voice.)* Yaw-hi toy ong traw lie taw!! *(The wind blows, kicking up a dust, the sky darkens, there is a stroke of lightning and a clap of thunder.)* YAW-HI TOY ONG TRAW LIE TAW! HI MANN KONN CHAW KOO ONG DUN TAW! DUN DAY ONG TOAT! [Wind — blow him back to me. Bring his dog to me. Don't let him get away!]

GENEVA.   Mr. Fellers! *(In a second stroke of lightning we can see that Lyman is back. The wind abates but it is still dark.)*

LYMAN.   I don't know no more. I don't know things.

GERI.   I don't care. *(The sky clears some, a dim setting sun slants horizontally through the trees.)*

LYMAN.   I didn't ask you to talk to me; I don't want people talking to me. I don't know how to be with people. Don't expect things from me. I got nothing for you. I got nothing for you.

GERI.   *(Soothing.)* I know.

LYMAN.   He wanted to die, he died, let him die.

GERI.   Nobody ever dies in my culture. You're always there.

LYMAN.   Don't talk to me anymore. I don't know nothing more about him.

GERI.   Lyman, I don't worry about Laird anymore.

LYMAN.   I don't know how to talk to people. I don't know how to be with people.

GERI.   *(She takes his hand.)* You have a very strong constitution. You're very healthy to spend so much time exposed to the elements. They've been good to you.

LYMAN.   I don't want nothing from you.

GERI.   One of the first pieces Laird taught me was a piece I'd like to play for you. You probably heard him play it. It was one of his favorites. Maybe because he said he was related to the composer. If that's true, then I guess I'm related to him too. His name was Erik Alfred Leslie Satie; he was the spiritual godfather of *les six* in Paris. He wrote a piece as he imagined the gymnasts, back in Greece had done their exercises to, when they were preparing for the Olympics. Daddy liked the idea of a girl playing it because women weren't allowed to watch the original Olympics. The athletes performed naked. *(She continues to hold his hand and raises her other arm in the air. The set slowly begins to return to the music room. They will be standing in the doorway when the change is complete.)* Any woman who saw them, even accidentally, was immediately put to death. You have to imagine the naked men, all very serious, standing on a green hill performing a series of exercises that look almost like a dance; very slowly in time to the music. They have incredible concentration, and they all move together in perfect synchronization. *(She has let go of his hand. He remains standing in the doorway, watching her. Geneva watches as Geri moves to the piano and begins to play the slow, steady* Gymnopedies* *by Satie. After a long moment, as she plays, concentrating completely on her work, Lyman moves a step into the room and sits on one of the straight back chairs. The music continues for a moment before the lights fade to black.)*

CURTAIN

* See Special Note on Songs and Recordings on copyright page.

PROPERTY LIST

Knapsack (LYMAN) with:
    bamboo papers for joint
Purse (GERI) with:
    wallet containing license, money, many pictures
Dog tags (LYMAN)
Cup of coffee (GERI)
Map (GERI)
Spoon
Sugar

SOUND EFFECTS

Thunder roll
Birds call
Eagle call
Door slam
Twig snapping
Dog barking
Car doors slam

NEW PLAYS

• **MERE MORTALS by David Ives, author of _All in the Timing_.** Another critically acclaimed evening of one-act comedies combining wit, satire, hilarity and intellect -- a winning combination. The entire evening of plays can be performed by 3 men and 3 women. ISBN: 0-8222-1632-9

• **BALLAD OF YACHIYO by Philip Kan Gotanda.** A provocative play about innocence, passion and betrayal, set against the backdrop of a Hawaiian sugar plantation in the early 1900s. _"Gotanda's writing is superb ... a great deal of fine craftsmanship on display here, and much to enjoy."_ --Variety. _"...one of the country's most consistently intriguing playwrights..."_ --San Francisco Examiner. _"As he has in past plays, Gotanda defies expectations..."_ --Oakland Tribune. [3M, 4W] ISBN: 0-8222-1547-0

• **MINUTES FROM THE BLUE ROUTE by Tom Donaghy.** While packing up a house, a family converges for a weekend of flaring tempers and shattered illusions. _"With MINUTES FROM THE BLUE ROUTE [Donaghy] succeeds not only in telling a story -- a typically American one with wide appeal, about how parents and kids struggle to understand each other and mostly fail -- but in notating it inventively, through wittily elliptical, crisscrossed speeches, and in making it carry a fairly vast amount of serious weight with surprising ease."_ --Village Voice. [2M, 2W] ISBN: 0-8222-1608-6

• **SCAPIN by Molière, adapted by Bill Irwin and Mark O'Donnell.** This adaptation of Molière's 325-year-old farce, _Les Fourberies de Scapin_, keeps the play in period while adding a late Twentieth Century spin to the language and action. _"This SCAPIN, [with a] felicitous adaptation by Mark O'Donnell, would probably have gone over big with the same audience who first saw Molière's Fourberies de Scapin...in Paris in 1671."_ --N.Y. Times. _"Commedia dell'arte and vaudeville have at least two things in common: baggy pants and Bill Irwin. All make for a natural fit in the celebrated clown's entirely unconventional adaptation."_ --Variety [9M, 3W, flexible] ISBN: 0-8222-1603-5

• **THE TURN OF THE SCREW adapted for the stage by Jeffrey Hatcher from the story by Henry James.** The American master's classic tale of possession is given its most interesting "turn" yet: one woman plays the mansion's terrified governess while a single male actor plays everyone else. _"In his thoughtful adaptation of Henry James' spooky tale, Jeffrey Hatcher does away with the supernatural flummery, exchanging the story's balanced ambiguities about the nature of reality for a portrait of psychological vampirism..."_ --Boston Globe. [1M, 1W] ISBN: 0-8222-1554-3

• **NEVILLE'S ISLAND by Tim Firth.** A middle management orientation exercise turns into an hilarious disaster when the team gets "shipwrecked" on an uninhabited island. _"NEVILLE'S ISLAND ... is that rare event: a genuinely good new play..., it's a comedic, adult LORD OF THE FLIES..."_ --The Guardian. _"... A non-stop, whitewater deluge of comedy both sophisticated and slapstick.... Firth takes a perfect premise and shoots it to the extreme, flipping his fish out of water, watching them flop around a bit, and then masterminding the inevitable feeding frenzy."_ --New Mexican. [4M] ISBN: 0-8222-1581-0

DRAMATISTS PLAY SERVICE, INC.
440 Park Avenue South, New York, NY 10016 212-683-8960 Fax 212-213-1539
postmaster@dramatists.com www.dramatists.com

NEW PLAYS

• **TAKING SIDES** by Ronald Harwood. Based on the true story of one of the world's greatest conductors whose wartime decision to remain in Germany brought him under the scrutiny of a U.S. Army determined to prove him a Nazi. *"A brave, wise and deeply moving play delineating the confrontation between culture, and power, between art and politics, between irresponsible freedom and responsible compromise." --London Sunday Times.* [4M, 3W] ISBN: 0-8222-1566-7

• **MISSING/KISSING** by John Patrick Shanley. Two biting short comedies, MISSING MARISA and KISSING CHRISTINE, by one of America's foremost dramatists and the Academy Award winning author of *Moonstruck.* *" ... Shanley has an unusual talent for situations ... and a sure gift for a kind of inner dialogue in which people talk their hearts as well as their minds...." --N.Y. Post.* MISSING MARISA [2M], KISSING CHRISTINE [1M, 2W] ISBN: 0-8222-1590-X

• **THE SISTERS ROSENSWEIG** by Wendy Wasserstein, Pulitzer Prize-winning author of *The Heidi Chronicles.* Winner of the 1993 Outer Critics Circle Award for Best Broadway Play. A captivating portrait of three disparate sisters reuniting after a lengthy separation on the eldest's 50th birthday. *"The laughter is all but continuous." --New Yorker.* *"Funny. Observant. A play with wit as well as acumen.... In dealing with social and cultural paradoxes, Ms. Wasserstein is, as always, the most astute of commentators." --N.Y. Times.* [4M, 4W] ISBN: 0-8222-1348-6

• **MASTER CLASS** by Terrence McNally. Winner of the 1996 Tony Award for Best Play. Only a year after winning the Tony Award for *Love! Valour! Compassion!,* Terrence McNally scores again with the most celebrated play of the year, an unforgettable portrait of Maria Callas, our century's greatest opera diva. *"One of the white-hot moments of contemporary theatre. A total triumph." --N.Y. Post.* *"Blazingly theatrical." -- USA Today.* [3M, 3W] ISBN: 0-8222-1521-7

• **DEALER'S CHOICE** by Patrick Marber. A weekly poker game pits a son addicted to gambling against his own father, who also has a problem but won't admit it. *"... make tracks to DEALER'S CHOICE, Patrick Marber's wonderfully masculine, razor-sharp dissection of poker-as-life.... It's a play that comes out swinging and never lets up -- a witty, wisecracking drama that relentlessly probes the tortured souls of its six very distinctive ... characters. CHOICE is a cutthroat pleasure that you won't want to miss." --Time Out (New York).* [6M] ISBN: 0-8222-1616-7

• **RIFF RAFF** by Laurence Fishburne. RIFF RAFF marks the playwriting debut of one of Hollywood's most exciting and versatile actors. *"Mr. Fishburne is surprisingly and effectively understated, with scalding bubbles of anxiety breaking through the surface of a numbed calm." --N.Y. Times.* *"Fishburne has a talent and a quality...[he] possesses one of the vital requirements of a playwright -- a good ear for the things people say and the way they say them." --N.Y. Post.* [3M] ISBN: 0-8222-1545-4

DRAMATISTS PLAY SERVICE, INC.
440 Park Avenue South, New York, NY 10016 212-683-8960 Fax 212-213-1539
postmaster@dramatists.com www.dramatists.com